Delight Directed Learning

Guide Your Homeschooler
Toward Passionate Learning

Lee Binz,
The HomeScholar

First Printing, 2015

Printed in the United States of America

Cover Design by Robin Montoya
Edited by Kimberly Charron

ISBN: 150898767X
ISBN-13: 978-1508987673

Disclaimer: Parents assume full responsibility for the education of their children in accordance with state law. College requirements vary, so make sure to check with the colleges about specific requirements for homeschoolers. We offer no guarantees, written or implied, that the use of our products and services will result in college admissions or scholarship awards.

Delight Directed Learning

Guide Your Homeschooler Toward Passionate Learning

What are Coffee Break Books?

Delight Directed Learning is part of The HomeScholar's Coffee Break Book series.

Designed especially for parents who don't want to spend hours and hours reading a 400-page book on homeschooling high school, each book combines Lee's practical and friendly approach with detailed, but easy-to-digest information, perfect to read over a cup of coffee at your favorite coffee shop!

Never overwhelming, always accessible and manageable, each book in the series will give parents the tools they need to tackle the tasks of homeschooling high school, one warm sip at a time.

Everything about these Coffee Break Books is designed to suggest simplicity, ease and comfort—from the size (fits in a purse), to the font and paragraph length (easy on the eyes), to the price (the same as a Starbucks Venti Triple Caramel Macchiato). Unlike a fancy coffee drink, however, these books are guilt-free pleasures you will want to enjoy again and again!

Table of Contents

Introduction

Not Just for Unschoolers Anymore!

When homeschoolers think of delight directed learning, they usually think of it as any specialization their children pursue independently. When colleges talk about this attribute, they call it passion. If you've read any articles in "U.S. News & World Report" discussing how colleges want to see passion, they're talking about delight directed learning.

Although parents may often call their child's chosen specialization frustrating, boring, or annoying, it's clear that colleges consider it a desirable asset when they evaluate student applications. Your child's interests and passions will make them stand out in the crowd of cookie-cutter college applicants, and will lead to greater success at earning college admission and scholarships. It used to be that delight directed learning was just for unschoolers. This is no longer the case!

Delight directed learning occurs when a child is given the space to pursue a topic because they take great delight in it, and not merely because it's required for a course. From a homeschooler's perspective, delight directed learning is important to foster a love of learning and a lifelong learning style in children, so they can become people who can adapt to any situation. The more the world changes, the more we need lifelong learners to make sense of it all. Sometimes, this kind of learning can involve unit studies on the topic your child loves. Other times, delight directed learning might be called self-study, with your child pursuing their interests and passions outside their regular homeschool curriculum.

One of the great advantages of delight directed learning is that it can improve your teenager's ability to cooperate. If your teen is more involved and tuned in to what they are studying, they won't get as burned out as they might doing what doesn't interest them. Pursuing their delight can make learning more meaningful; when they apply learning to something they care about, education makes more sense, and they take ownership of it.

Delight can give you both inspiration for core classes and fill your high school transcript with electives. It gives colleges exactly what they want to see from teenagers—passion, an interest that lasts for years. Colleges prefer to see interests that last throughout high school, because this indicates an ability to succeed over a long period of time.

The only way to accomplish four years of the same activity without fighting with your teenager is if it's an activity your teenager wants to do! This book will show you how to identify, nurture, and record your child's delight. It will lead your child to greater success at earning college admission and scholarships.

Chapter 1

How Can I Figure Out My Child's Passion?

For many parents, trying to figure out what their teenager is interested in can be an exercise in frustration. Many teens only seem to be passionate about video games or social media! But every child has a special interest, gift, ability, or passion; it simply takes time to figure it out.

The 2004 Pixar film *The Incredibles* has much to teach us concerning raising our children, specifically, how to nurture and develop the "super" abilities that lie dormant within each of them. That's right, each of them. I firmly believe each of our children is a budding superhero waiting to be discovered and developed.

Their abilities and passions are likely not as dramatic as our fictional friends, but that does not diminish the potential of each of our kids to change the world in their own way.

In this film, a couple of former superheroes, Mr. Incredible and Elastigirl, get married. Because of a class-action lawsuit against all superheroes, they are forced deep undercover using the alter–egos, Bob and Helen Parr. The movie explores how this true power couple deals with suppressing their superpowers to live a "normal" life.

One of the most intriguing aspects of this film is how Bob and Helen deal with their children, two of whom have nascent superpowers. Their aptly named son, Dash, has super-speed. His older sister, Violet, has the ability to become invisible and cast force fields. The baby of the family, Jack Jack, has not displayed any super-powers, and the family is slowly accepting the possibility that he is not super at all.

Jack Jack's Story

Baby Jack Jack is a mystery. His parents must realize he has to be "special." He has the right DNA, yet he displays no superpowers. There is absolutely nothing his mom and dad can do to force superpowers into him. All they can do is wait and watch. This is one of our primary roles as homeschooling parents. Gifts are discovered, not created. We need to be students of our students to discover the secrets that lie deep within.

Eventually, Jack Jack's superpowers are hilariously revealed to an unsuspecting babysitter. Similarly, you may be surprised by the gifts your children display. Even the most normal kids often reveal themselves as "super" in one or more areas of their lives. In our family, our kids' gifts revealed themselves in areas we would never have imagined.

Kevin's Story

Our oldest son exhibited a sudden and profound talent in chess at fourteen years old. Chess was something we taught our kids when they were five and seven. We taught them in the loosest sense of the word, simply how the pieces move and no more. This lesson lay dormant in my eldest for years. For his fourteenth birthday, Kevin requested a chess book. I looked at him as if he had requested Adam Smith's *The Wealth of Nations*. I was clueless as to where this desire came from. None of our ancestors played chess and we had not played nor spoken of it for years.

On his birthday, he received many presents, but only one made it back to his room that day, *Play Winning Chess* by Yasser Seirawan. Kevin emerged from his room about two weeks later and proclaimed, "I'm ready to play in a tournament." Before acceding to this, my husband told Kevin he would have to beat his dad first. I detected the slightest trace of a smile on his face as Kevin quickly ripped Matt's position apart and stomped enthusiastically on his king. After that, we were quite willing to let him pick on someone more his intellectual size, so off to a chess tournament we went.

The tournament director looked at my husband with disdain. He was convinced my husband was one of those parents who pushed his children too hard to hide his own shortcomings. However, a few minutes of interrogation convinced him that chess was probably the least likely place my husband would choose to bolster his self-esteem. Matt was utterly lost. Kevin, however, felt right at home. He ripped through a series of adult opponents with enthusiasm normally reserved for a box of Krispy Kremes. He left his first tournament with a provisional rating that placed him among the elite of Washington State high school chess players, almost all of whom had professional coaches and had competed for years.

We spent the next four years feeding our son chess books and driving him to tournaments. He completed his high school chess career by finishing second in state, not bad for a late starting, self-taught chess player with no documented chess DNA.

Alex's Story

A couple of years after my eldest's surprise birthday request, my youngest son did, in fact, ask me for Adam Smith's *The Wealth of Nations*. Again, we never saw it coming. My husband and I both hated economics. I failed economics in college. Both of us were nonplussed at this request. *The Wealth of Nations* was followed by *Democracy in America* and various other ancient tomes on political economics and philosophy. We learned not to ask too many "why" questions, and simply forked over the books. We figured it was a good investment.

That is exactly the way it turned out. For reasons known only to God, my youngest son had caught fire for economics. This led to amazing opportunities for him, with scholarships, fellowships, and meaningful employment, none of which would have been possible if we had attempted to force his passion into areas where we, his parents, felt more comfortable.

Such is the nature of children and superheroes. Who they are and what they become may not be what you think. It may not even be in the realm of imagination. In fact, with Kevin and Alex, the only way it made any sense at all was in retrospect. Kevin had always been quiet and analytical as a child, so looking back now, chess seems a somewhat logical source of his enchantment. Alex was always our little academic, so philosophy made some sense in hindsight. However, we still scratch our heads over his interest in economics.

The Message

Be students of your students. Observe their passions. Don't be too skeptical or try to force them to love what you love. They are individuals and will spend their lives striving to become who God intended. You play a critical role in shaping and guiding, but not in defining or forcing. Some of your children may exhibit "superpowers" in chess, math, economics, and philosophy. Others will flex their muscles in sports, writing, dance, or music. I have encountered children who demonstrate leadership in areas as diverse as acting, mycology, and fiddling. The first step in raising your own superheroes is to discover where their superpowers reside. It will require your most focused attention and will frequently demand that most elusive of all superpowers, patience.

You can do it. The world needs them, and your superheroes are counting on you!

Chapter 2

Providing Opportunity

In order to help your child find an activity they are passionate about, you must give them opportunities to explore.

Finding Their Passion

Many homeschool schedules are full of homework, chores, outside classes, and work, and there isn't much time for students to explore their interests. It's important to allow margin in your student's life, so they have enough time in the day to pursue what they want to do and not only what *you* want them to do.

Sometimes, opportunity can mean providing your child with a broad array of courses, so they can find an interest.

If your student doesn't seem interested in anything, providing a liberal arts education will expose them to many different possibilities. For instance, they may discover a love of theater through taking a speech or debate class, or an interest in zoology through a marine science course. Variety may be the key for students who don't seem to have any specific interests yet.

You can also search curriculum catalogs together and see what books and curriculum your child seems to love. My son *asked* for Sonlight American Government when he was young, merely because he was interested. Let your child look in the catalog and watch videos, while you listen for clues about how to get involved while your child is simply enjoying the content.

Providing opportunity might also mean doing school work only four days a week. This can sound shocking to some people, but it's what we did in our homeschool. I did school work with my children for four days a week, and the fifth day was their time for delight directed learning.

Fanning the Flames

Providing opportunity also means finding ways for your child to pursue their passion once they've discovered it. Of course, this also means you have to go with your child, drive them, wait for them, and all the other inconvenient things parents do to encourage their children's interests. Sorry about that! I got to be good friends with my barista during those years of my life!

One way to encourage your child's interest is to find them a mentor in the area of their delight. Try doing a Google search for their interest, such as "ornithology club" to find a group for your child. You can also find mentors by contacting small, friendly colleges in search of a helpful professor. Ask around at church and other community groups to see if you can find an adult with the same interests.

It took a *long* time asking before we found an economics mentor for our son. The first two we tried weren't a good fit, but they eventually led to a great professor who took our son under his wing. Ask yourself, if this was your interest now, as an adult, how would *you* find a way to meet like-minded people?

If you have a child who is on fire for a specific topic, keeping up with them can be exhausting! Keeping my son Kevin away from his chessboard was about as easy as keeping my dog away from his dinner bowl. Our Brittany Spaniel, Bailey, would have pulled against his collar until unconscious if I ever tried to hold him back from dinner. Kids often show similar determination, but their approach is not nearly as linear. Indeed, children will happily employ all of their creativity finding ways to do what they want when you're not looking. It got to the point where we could not even ask Kevin to clean the playroom without supervision, because that was where his true love (the chess board) resided.

Passion demands opportunity if it is to flourish. I believe parents have the responsibility to have our kids near the door when opportunity comes a-knockin'. The questions to pay attention to here are:

1) How do you recognize and evaluate opportunities for your kid?
2) How can you know which doors to open and which ones to lock shut?

One of the strongest a-ha moments in raising our youngest came when he was twelve. Shortly after we moved, he read something in the newspaper that irritated him. I believe it was an editorial about tax policy, understandably not a normal concern for a twelve-year-old boy. He asked permission and we agreed to let him write a letter to the newspaper editor. A couple of days later, we got a call from the editor asking to speak to Alex. The editor wanted to verify that Alex had written the letter and that he was indeed twelve. It was obvious they were checking to make sure these weren't parental thoughts planted into a child's head. We laughed because we rarely understood what Alex said, let alone placed thoughts in his head. They printed the letter.

Of course, that wasn't the end of the story. About a week later, I went to the mailbox and found an anonymous post card that was disturbing and vaguely threatening. It was addressed to Alex and cautioned him to stop lying about writing the letter when it was "obvious" that a parent had written it for him. The writer went on to say how Alex would ruin his life if he continued to "pretend" to pass off his parents' thoughts as his own. We discussed the post card, and decided not to tell Alex about it until he got older. The world is scary enough without having to deal with anonymous, misguided "do-gooders" trying to teach your children ethics!

In the long-term, we gleaned one important lesson from this episode: Don't show the newspaper to your children .... no, that wasn't it ... never underestimate your children, that's the one! As parents, we tend to have certain expectations of kids' behavior at certain ages. It is true that in many ways, Alex was a typical twelve-year-old boy; he loved baseball, swimming, and playing world domination games. However, in his area of passion, he was well advanced in both maturity and ability.

In this instance, the door of opportunity was easy to recognize, an opportunity to publish his letter in the city newspaper. Some parents might have missed the door, by wrongly assuming a twelve-year-old could have nothing important to say. Over the years, Alex's passion about economics led us to many doors, some of them much bigger and (as parents) much scarier. This first door was easy though, all we had to say was, "OK, open it."

In our family, Matt and I agreed to encourage any passions our kids demonstrated. This did not mean, however, that we didn't have a lot of false starts. At various times, our kids were into architecture, interior design, aviation, and computers. Our garage sales are still filled with relics of these misadventures. We once observed Kevin coaching a five-year old in a chess concept and were completely convinced he was going to be a teacher. He displayed the tenderness and patience of a young Mr. Rogers. While teaching as a career is not likely in Kevin's future (he's not analytical enough), he has managed to parlay his good-natured demeanor into a rewarding vocation as a chess coach.

The key is a commitment on the part of parents to understand their children, to recognize how God built them, and to identify and provide opportunities to develop their gifts. Homeschooling is the perfect environment to discover these gifts because you can observe your children in many different environments and learning situations. In public school, you are likely to miss some of these aha moments, simply because you are not there to witness them.

Even if your speculations don't pan out, these interactions are a valuable component of your child's growth. In our home, we often played the game of "Catch the Kids Doing Something Right." We would observe them doing something new and say, "I see you were being very tender and sweet teaching chess to that little boy" or "I noticed you really enjoyed teaching Sunday School class." These interactions did not necessarily lead to instant self-actualization in the kids, but they did reinforce ideas they were forming about themselves.

Kevin heard so frequently that he was kind, gentle, loving, and tender, that he eventually incorporated this into his self-image. We are convinced it is one reason he is a tremendous husband and will be a great father. Since he was young, Alex heard his ideas were important and needed to be shared. He believes this about himself and it will enable him to be a strong leader.

It is important that your observations are not only flattery or wishful thinking, but based on real events. True self-esteem is always built on real accomplishments and not simply on an egalitarian desire that everyone is special. As that little sage, Dash, said in *The Incredibles*, "When everyone is special, no one is." Kids aren't dumb. They know the difference between getting a trophy for participating in little league and getting one for being MVP.

Being "special" outside of accomplishment cheapens real achievement.

Do you ever wonder how the military can take young men and women, some of whom have very little by way of obvious gifts, and in a short time produce self-confident, mature citizens? I believe a significant component of this transformation is that recruits are given the responsibility to perform real, meaningful work. In the military, accomplishment is recognized in a meaningful way, while mediocrity and indifference are discouraged (usually with extreme prejudice).

As homeschool parents, we should also strive to give our kids something meaningful to do. In our family, we did school work four days a week. In the early years, the fifth day was for visits to the park, book report lunches, or play dates with friends. When they became teens, however, Friday was reserved for finding a real job and pursuing their areas of passion.

For Kevin, this meant demonstrating his maturity and chess skills to a National Chess Master, Elliott Neff, and getting hired as a chess coach in area schools. For Alex, this meant communicating his economics knowledge to the leadership of Discovery Institute in Seattle and becoming a research intern.

While as parents, we all believe our kids are special, how we communicate this idea to our children is critically important. Praising kids for mediocre performance or for simply trying, without the companion commitment necessary to achieve excellence, will lead to a generation of narcissistic, self-indulgent adults.

While our family enjoys the hit TV show *American Idol*, we intentionally miss the early episodes each season because we can't bear to watch the pathetic parade of hopefuls being filleted by the judges. What would possess young people, who I'm sure are perfectly competent in other areas of their lives, to publicly display their deficiencies in front of millions of viewers? My guess is that as children they overdosed on the two unconditional affirmations from the Cult of Self Esteem: "You are special" and "You can do anything."

But is it responsible, is it kind to feed such pabulum to children? Remember, the parent's role is to help children discover the gifts God has placed within them, and then to shape and mold their kids as they grow into those gifts. Not every child is given every gift.

The process of catching fire can take years and, to be honest, most homeschool parents will not be able to point to a single event in their children's lives that lit the fire. Whether it is by lightning or by rubbing two little sticks together, a homeschool parent's job is to keep the tinder dry and gently fan even the smallest spark until it sets ablaze.

Chapter 3

Grading Delight Directed Learning and Covering the Core

Many of the homeschool parents I consult with are anxious about assigning grades for their children's schoolwork. When faced with the need to give a grade for delight directed learning, they often freeze. How do you give a grade for a course when you don't give any tests?

The key is to think about how you *do* evaluate your children. Just between you and me, the ways we evaluate are often the same things we nag about. Consider these phrases: "Are you done with your reading yet?" (Literature Reading, 100%.) "Have you finished your spelling words yet?" (Spelling Practice, 100%). Sometimes, what we nag them *not* to do is a good way to evaluate delight directed learning. For example, "Kevin, will you *please* leave that chessboard alone!" (Daily Chess Practice, 100%) or "Alex, get away from the piano!" (Piano Practice, 100%).

As you think about how to evaluate delight directed learning, consider everything your child does that you call school. In our homeschool, I only graded tests in math, foreign language, and science. (This was mainly a matter of convenience for me as that curriculum came with tests!) For all 28 of our other classes, I used other ways to evaluate my children, both for the core and delight directed classes. If they met my expectations, they received 100 percent.

To aid in your evaluation, look at the projects your child has completed. Perhaps they've read some books on their chosen subject and you can collect the book titles. Record any individual tasks they have completed, such as creating signs, developing a website, or writing to their legislator.

Another method is to write down the different steps in the learning process. Record the five different steps your child had to work through in order to present the debate for their speech and debate class. List each performance or piece they presented, or write down every display they made, and use it all as part of your grading scheme.

If your student is studying for the SAT or the ACT, and is practicing for the 25-minute essay section, instead of using a book of essay prompts, have them write a quick essay on the topic of their delight directed learning. This way, you have a piece of paper they've worked on that looks like schoolwork—a quick essay for English. It also becomes a way for you to document their delight directed learning. This piece of paper becomes their homework or test for the class.

As another example, if your child is passionate about a sport, give a grade for their experience. Include such factors as individual skills, teamwork, team skills, daily practice, and physical fitness as part of your grading criteria.

Homeschool grading is an art, not a science. There's no one right way to do it, as long as you capture their delight and give them honest credit for learning accomplished.

Covering Core Classes with Delight Directed Learning

At this point, you might be asking, "Delight directed learning is fine for electives, but what about the core courses?" The good news is you can even cover some core classes using your child's delight directed learning. I once heard a mom say, "My son's interested in something that's not a real academic course, he's mapping the moons of Jupiter." Another mom once told me, "I really need to teach my child music, because all he ever does is play bluegrass, and bluegrass isn't real music." I almost laughed out loud! Bluegrass is music, and mapping the moons of Jupiter is astronomy, and both are core courses required for college admission. They aren't standard music and science courses, but as homeschoolers, we can move beyond standard public school fare!

For example, you need to teach English for four years of high school as part of the core curriculum colleges want to see on a transcript. However, this doesn't mean you have to cover English in a regimented way. Depending on your child's interests, you might choose to cover English through courses such as poetry, creative writing, journalism, science fiction, or sports communication.

Perhaps your child is interested in early American literature, or African-American literature, or Shakespeare's works. They might be interested in a speech and debate class, an expository writing class, or social issues literature. You could even cover English with novel writing or Russian literature, like my sons did.

Consider the core course of science. If you cover science with delight directed learning, it might include a class on astronomy, geology, ornithology, or mycology, if your child has an interest in these areas. Science doesn't have to include the standard biology, chemistry, and physics, although these courses can be important, too.

Teach your children to read, write, and speak confidently. Teach them to do math quickly, accurately, and easily. This is your goal so your children are prepared for life.

Consider planning your middle school and high school courses. A rough draft with a five or six-year plan can eliminate some of the, "Oh, no! High school!" panic I sometimes see. Develop a plan that includes English, math, science, and social studies each year. Consider beginning foreign language study in middle school so your child can ease into it, allowing for plenty of time for the two to three years of foreign language many colleges require.

Chapter 4

Putting Delight Directed Learning on the Transcript

Can you create a serious-looking high school transcript that includes delight directed learning? After all, it's not book learning, so how should it look? What do you call all the different courses?

My son, Alex, was a self-motivated extreme learner. If only this was an Olympic event, like extreme sports! He learned to write a novel for fun and wanted to take a third year of French, even though I didn't have a curriculum for him. He asked for an American government curriculum for Christmas, and read every economics book he could get his hands on. Although his educational love language is reading, he was still a delight directed learner. When it was time to make his transcript, I had to figure out how to translate his experiences onto paper.

For our family, the problem seemed huge. What could I do with all these experiences that covered a wide range of subjects? Should the report on Jean-Baptiste Say (the French economist) be counted as history, economics, or foreign language? Was my son, Kevin's enjoyment of Russian History merely part of World History, or could it be a course by itself? My children wrote *so* many papers but I didn't know where I should file each of them!

The Sticky Note Strategy

I eventually found a system that helped me sort out all my children's delight directed learning, using my understanding of traditional grades and credits. Once I figured out a system, I realized it would work for *all* delight directed learners, not only book learners. My strategy is simple, fun, and only requires one small purchase—sticky notes. These small square notes save the day again! You can determine what to do with each delight directed educational experience using a simple sticky note.

Save each one with your homeschool records. At the end of each year, group your sticky notes together, and combine them to create high school courses.

I recognize it can be difficult to determine where each experience will fall on a transcript, so keep each sticky note simple. For each activity your student is involved in, there are five pieces of information you need to record on a sticky note. On each note, indicate the following items.

Name the Experience

What did you do? For instance, "Perform in Nutcracker." Do you have any course title ideas? Add, "Theater Arts: Performance." Simply guess and add as many ideas as you can on each sticky note!

Note the Year

In what year was this done? Sometimes it will be a school year, 20xx-20xy and other times it will be for a short duration, such as a play in November of 20xx.

Grade the Experience

Did your student complete the project or activity to your expectations? Were they successful, did they receive positive feedback or learn something? Remember that you don't have to test in order to give a grade.

Note Credits Earned or Hours Spent

Count or estimate the number of hours spent on the project or activity. A total of 75 to 90 hours can be recorded as a half credit. If your child accumulates more than 180 hours, you can consider it a very full credit, or choose to divide up the experiences into smaller, bite-sized pieces and then regroup them into other courses with 180 hours apiece. If there are less than 75 hours, you will be grouping the sticky notes together. Keep sticky notes for each activity, even when it required few hours. You can use all your child's experiences.

Suggest Possible Subject Areas

You may not know which subject you will assign for each experience, but you can record the possibilities. I often put several ideas on each note for papers and reports. One paper might be regarded as English, history, economics, or French. By making a note of it, I could decide later which course needed this experience to make up a full credit. If history was already packed, then I could use it for another subject area.

Spread Out and Group Together

Don't review your sticky notes until you are sitting down to work on the transcript. Checking them too often can cause frustration and insecurity, so only review them when you update your transcript each year. This will help you keep the big picture in mind. When you are ready to work on your transcript, spread all the sticky notes on the table or floor. Then place them into "affinity groups" (groups of similar things). As you combine activities, work to combine them into groups that ultimately add up to one credit or half credit subjects.

Once you have made a decision, put the course on your transcript. Make a note of the experiences you included on the transcript, if you want, which will help you write course descriptions as part of your homeschool records. But once you've decided on a credit, try not to stress about it again. It's easy enough to change if you need to, but putting experiences into groups is a success in itself. You have successfully grouped your delight directed learning into high school level courses!

This whole process of spreading notes out on the floor and manually grouping and regrouping experiences is a great technique for any parent who is a kinesthetic learner. Even if you don't use a hands-on curriculum, this hands-on transcript process can help you understand the nuances of your child's transcript. The process can ultimately help you remember what was included in each course and even help you write your course descriptions!

The "Testing" Strategy

Parents don't always know what their children are learning. There is so much life that goes on and so many books! It's amazing what children will learn when we aren't looking! Another way to quantify delight directed learning is to give subject tests. This doesn't work for every subject or every child, but it's an option to consider. Instead of testing your child as they are learning, you allow them to learn a subject naturally. When they are done, you can give them a sample test from a major test provider. If they pass the sample test at home or at the testing center, you will know how much they have learned, and will have a grade to put on their transcript. There are three tests available that will help you with this strategy: SAT Subject Tests, Advanced Placement (AP) exams, and College Level Exam Program (CLEP) tests.

When using tests to document delight directed learning, be sure to avoid the possibility of failure. Purchase a book with sample tests in it and give the exam at home first. Only take your student to an official test if you are reasonably sure they can pass. Your goal is to find out what they have learned, not to demonstrate what they have *not* learned. For more information on SAT Subject Tests, AP exams, or the CLEP test, go to the College Board website at www.CollegeBoard.org.

Finding Balance

To homeschool high school effectively, include as much delight directed learning as possible. A fun learning environment may not make school easy, but it does make it interesting and applicable. When school is interesting, children will learn more and they will *love* learning.

Parents need to find a balance, however. College preparation means you must also cover the core classes. When planning your week, first be sure to cover the core classes of reading, writing, math, science, and social studies. Each family will have classes they consider non-negotiable, core classes. Try to teach them in an interesting way. It's possible to teach many core subjects using delight directed classes, but make sure you cover the core one way or another.

Once the core is covered, capture your child's delights. Translate them into courses on your transcript. You don't have to plan, direct, or evaluate learning with tests or quizzes; simply capture learning.

Chapter 5

Writing Course Descriptions for Delight Directed Learning

Course descriptions for delight directed learning classes are written in the same way as regular course descriptions. Each should include a paragraph about what the student did (even though you weren't telling them what to do), as well as a list of things they used to learn. Include how you evaluated them.

First, write what your child used. In the example below (from my son Alex), you will see that he learns best through reading. If your child learns best through reading, simply follow along behind them and keep a list of the books they read. Remember that in school, they don't always use the *whole* book, sometimes they only read excerpts. If your student is not a book learner, then what did they use to learn the material? An instrument with sheet music? A series of computer programs or skills? A variety of techniques or media?

Second, write what your child accomplished. Alex didn't do much more than reading or writing in this example, but for other courses this will be a major portion of your explanation. Accomplishments may include performances, activities, and field trips—anything that you have to pay for or put on your calendar. For example, in art, I listed Alex's performances and the musical or theatrical events we attended.

Third, determine how you evaluated what your student did. Particularly with delight directed learning, it's important you don't attempt to assign tests to evaluate your child. This is about delight, and anything you do that removes some of the delight can slow your child down. Instead, think about it this way, "How do I know he has learned economics, piano, claymation, ornithology, or culinary arts?" Write each way of evaluating on your list.

Finally, write the course description. Remember that it's a simple paragraph at a fifth grade writing level. The chance of someone reading it in detail is relatively slim. It will probably be skimmed over and doesn't have to be perfect! If you have trouble getting started, try giving yourself a simple writing prompt. "This is a self-directed course. In this course the student will ..."

Sample Course Description

Elective: Economics 1

This is a self-directed course. Studying a variety of books, the student will independently investigate economics.

The student will discuss his findings, and write one or more research papers on the topic of his choosing within that subject. Credit will be awarded based on 150 hours of study and research, and successful completion of a written report. Written work available on request.

Texts used:

- *Whatever Happened to Penny Candy?* by Richard Maybury
- *The Money Mystery* by Richard Maybury
- *The Clipper Ship Strategy* by Richard Maybury
- *Uncle Eric Talks About Personal, Career & Financial Security* by Richard Maybury
- *Investing for the Future* by Larry Burkett
- *Answers to Your Family's Financial Questions* by Larry Burkett
- *Money Matters for Teens* by Larry Burkett

- *Money Matters for Teens Workbook* age 15-18 Edition by Larry Burkett
- Biblical Economics in Comics by Vic Lockman
- *Money, Banking and Usury: A Biblical View* by Vic Lockman
- *How to Lie With Statistics* by Darrell Huff
- *Growing Money: A Complete Investing Guide for Kids* by Gail Karlitz
- *The Motley Fool Investment Guide by David and Tom Gardner*
- *Rich Dad Poor Dad* by Robert T. Kiyosaki
- *Rich Kid Smart Kid*: Giving Your Child a Financial Head Start by Robert T. Kiyosaki
- *The Unemotional Investor: Simple Systems for Beating the Market* by Robert Sheard
- *The Motley Food Investment Guide* by David and Tom Gardner

Excerpts from:

- *The Wealth of Nations* by Adam Smith
- *Applying Economics Principles* textbook by Sanford D. Gordon, published by Glencoe
- *Economics: The Way We Choose* by Paul W. Barkley, published by HBJ, Inc.
- *Basic Economics* by Clarence B. Carson

Course Grade

Economics 1

Completed 06/03

Reading	Analysis	Writing
1/3 grade	1/3 grade	1/3 grade

Reading 100%

Narration and Discussion 100%

Business Cycle Management 100%

Investment Guide 100%

Final grade for Economics 1 = 100% = A

A=90-100% =4.0

B=80-89% = 3.0

C=70-79% = 2.0

D = 60-69% = 1.0

Chapter 6

Physical Education Outside the Box

Teaching P.E. outside the box is one of the greatest joys of homeschooling. Whether your child is a current couch potato or destined for professional sports, all children can benefit from homeschool P.E. You can keep them always challenged, but never overwhelmed, by choosing the appropriate physical education experience for your child. Starting where they are, you can help them become more physically fit for the rest of their life, while also preparing them for college or career goals.

P.E. stands for "physical education," not only "physical exercise." You can create the perfect high school P.E. class for your child because it can be a helpful combination of education and exercise. After all, some kids are very active in sports, and all you have to do is count the hours they spend breaking a sweat. For kids who are not so active, it helps to think outside the box. Your child could take CPR classes or study health instead. Some kids who hate P.E. love swing-dancing or computer games requiring movement. Any physical activity that breaks a sweat counts!

College Requirements

Colleges and careers may require two to four years of P.E. in high school. Although many colleges don't require P.E., others expect to see P.E. classes, seeing it as a "socialization" issue. Some military careers, as well as military and police academies, want to see some proof of physical fitness. And if your child is into sports, the NCAA will expect to see P.E. classes on the transcript.

Children can earn P.E. credits without a curriculum. Be specific with class titles. Instead of calling the class "P.E." or "Physical Education," create a second name for your class that gives more information. A homeschool P.E. class might be called, "P.E.: Personal Fitness with Health," or "P.E.: Basketball and Soccer." Consider the wide variety of physical education options available, and then think outside the box!

Grades and Credits

There are two ways to count credits. One way is by using a standard textbook or curriculum, which is uncommon for P.E. class. The second way is by counting or estimating hours. One high school P.E. credit is 120 to 180 hours, and 60 to 90 hours is a half credit. If your child works on the class the whole school year, then that one hour per day is one whole credit, and half hour per day is a half credit. In general, it's best to give only one P.E. credit per year, even if your child racks up a huge numbers of hours.

P.E. grades are always subjective, even in public schools, but providing grades helps colleges understand your homeschool. You already evaluate P.E. in many ways, even if you don't realize it. You think about whether your child does the work (schools call it "attendance") their level of effort, demonstration of specific skills or teamwork, understanding of concepts, personal fitness goals achieved, and consider any reading or discussion. Estimate your child's grade, keeping in mind all these ways of evaluating.

A grade of *A* or 4.0 means the child shows mastery of your goals, meets your high expectations, or loves what they are doing. A grade of *B* or 3.0 means they did well, but it's definitely not worth an *A*. A grade of *C* or 2.0 means it was a bad experience, not good at all, but they did enough to meet your minimum requirements.

Physical Education

Your homeschool P.E. class could focus on education rather than exercise. A focus on education may be a good fit for bookish children. Choose a focus for the year, or mix and match unit studies together until your child has enough hours for one P.E. class.

Focus on Health

You could focus on health in your P.E. class. Check your state homeschool law, because sometimes health is a requirement for graduation, but it's unlikely your child needs a health credit every year of high school. We liked the health books by Susan Boe. Written for Christian Schools, these books assume the student lives in a reasonably healthy environment, without sex or drugs. They cover physical, spiritual, and social health.

For junior high or middle school, *Total Health: Talking About Life's Changes* by Susan Boe

For high school, *Total Health: Choices for a Winning Lifestyle* by Susan Boe

Focus on Relationships

Relationship and purity studies can be a health related topic as well. You can read and discuss issues about dating. Consider these popular books:

For younger teens, *Passport to Purity* by Dennis and Barbara Rainey

For older teens, age 14-19, *When God Writes Your Love Story* by Eric and Leslie Ludy

For young adults, *Boundaries in Dating* by Henry Cloud and John Townsend

Focus on Nutrition

Some families will research essential

oils, healing herbs, or other natural remedies. This study time could make up a nutrition course. There are excellent classes available from The Great Courses. You can focus on healthy eating with their course, Nutrition Made Clear.

Focus on First Aid

First aid, lifeguard, and CPR classes from the American Red Cross or your local fire station are a great addition to any P.E. class. As a registered nurse, I encourage all families to certify in CPR and maintain certification (yearly or so depending on your state). Your child's CPR certification becomes a way you can evaluate P.E. class.

Focus on Fitness

There are many ways to include fitness in everyday life. Look for opportunities to cover P.E. outside the box.

Personal Fitness

A personal fitness class can be as simple as counting everything that breaks a sweat. Yard work, manual labor, and playing basketball in the backyard all count as personal fitness. If you take fitness seriously in your family, you may want to include weight training, strength training, and cardio into your daily routine. Indoor or outdoor exercises count, and no gym membership or sports teams are necessary.

Teams and Socialization

Sports teams are a great way to collect P.E. hours, and it doesn't matter what kind of sports team your child is on. Sometimes teams will come with a rough social environment, of course. My children were involved in organized sports, making summer an interesting time. In a secular sports league, they were exposed to some unsavory behavior and vocabulary. Because the exposure was limited, these issues didn't become part of my children's psyches. Instead, they could observe this behavior as if from a distance. We could discuss the negative socialization without them taking it on as a personality trait.

If your child is participating in team sports or sport camps, it can be an eye-opener for them. They can learn what socialization is like in school, but because it's not an all-day and all-year experience, and with appropriate "de-briefing" they are unlikely to face any negative consequences.

Individual Sports

From golf to running, there are many individual sports to choose from, some with a socialization component. Golf, for example, is a great opportunity for walking and talking together. Look into the First Tee program. First Tee provides young people of all backgrounds an opportunity to develop life-enhancing values such as confidence, perseverance, and judgment through golf and character education. First Tee offers wonderful college scholarships for participation, with a mission to promote healthy choices in teens. Read more about First Tee at thefirsttee.org.

Active Play

Summer is a great time for learning new skills—especially skills that count as P.E. Kids can learn skills such as bowling, swimming, ice skating, or inline skating. They might participate in a fun run, marathon, or walk-a-thon for charity to learn how to give. Gather a group of friends and enjoy day hikes, mid-day picnicking, or active outdoor games. Camping with family or friends can encourage great outdoor skills that count for P.E.

Kids who love to play more than

anything else are perfect candidates for learning real skills. On their own, they may learn new games, new sports, and try new skills with their friends. If you meet with other homeschoolers at a park, encourage everyone to bring outdoor games. Search your closets for badminton, croquet, bocce, or volleyball gear.

Bibliophiles

If your child loves books, you can pursue physical education by buying books to encourage physical fitness. Many books have detailed photos or drawings of exercises. For a child who hates exercise, you may want to try *8 Minutes in the Morning* by Jorge Cruise. It's a quick read, with some chapters on healthy living—diet, exercise, sleep, etc. There is a section describing exercises that can be completed in eight minutes a day.

Science minded children may enjoy the Charlotte Mason style of learning. A nature handbook or field guide may send them off to the wilderness, contentedly learning as they enjoy nature.

Dance

Artists may not gravitate toward soccer, but they may be involved in dance. Whether they love swing, ballroom, or ballet, anything that breaks a sweat can count as P.E., so dance certainly fits the bill. Young artists often have more than enough credits for fine arts, so it's easy to put their dance hours in the P.E. category.

Artistic Pursuits

If your artistic child is not a dancer, focus on the art they love. A bike, a backpack, and some art supplies may be all they need for a summer P.E. credit. They can hike or bike to a scenic vista to sketch, paint, or draw. New drawing supplies may be the only motivation needed!

An artist may also be drawn to musical concerts in the park. Find your park department schedule and determine if they hold music or theater performances. An artist might be convinced to spend time in the park playing Frisbee or soccer before performances, or enjoy the music while playing active games. Exercising with their favorite music might be just the ticket. For some, this means a stationary bicycle or jogging with classical music accompaniment.

Auditory Learners

Take advantage of the auditory learning style. Auditory learners may be motivated to do aerobics by downloading fast-paced music on their MP3 player or smartphone that they can enjoy while taking a walk. An auditory learner may find audio books so enjoyable that they will even go for long walks, hikes, or bike rides while listening to great literature. Be sure to include these books on their reading list, carefully labeled as audio books.

Outdoor Education

Whether shooting, hunting, or archery, there are many ways to include outdoor education in a P.E. class. Olympic sports, such as archery or shooting, can also be considered part of P.E. Camping, hiking, snowshoeing and other outdoor recreation would be an awesome addition. My Gold Care Club members are often involved in Boy Scouts and spend hundreds of hours doing outdoor activities each year. I suggest only creating one P.E. credit per year, and "Outdoor Education" might be a good title.

Techie Teens

Some teens are all about the computer. A computer-based option might be a good fit, as long as you carefully make sure your sweet child is moving while they play. Some of the gaming systems involving movement are Xbox One with Kinect, PlayStation 4 with Move controllers, and the Nintendo Switch.

Search for movement-based games if you already have a gaming console. Wii Fit U and Wii Sports Club are games for the older Wii U game console, which offers fitness games including yoga, strength, and stamina. On the PlayStation 4 (and previous consoles), you can play Just Dance. Dance, Dance Revolution is available for the computer using a USB-attachable soft dance pad. Xbox One (and previous consoles) has Nike+ Kinect Training and other fitness games. There are too many movement-based options to list. When choosing a computer-based interactive fitness game, look for one that helps the child elevate their heart rate. If they are only moving their arms, then it's not exercise or education ... it's merely a computer game. And be extremely careful to read ratings on any game before you purchase.

Physical Education Over-achievers

Sometimes parents focus so much on teaching P.E. that they forget what their children are already doing. If your child is already involved in a sport or scouting, then they are probably getting all the P.E. they need. But there are others who are over-achievers in the physical education area.

The Congressional Award

Kids who enjoy physical fitness may be motivated by The Congressional Award program. This program has four focus areas: Volunteer Public Service, Personal Development, Physical Fitness, and Expedition/Exploration. This is also a great way to be noticed by your congressman, if your child is interested in attending a military academy someday. Look into The Congressional Award to see if you can create a significant award out of P.E. for fun. Read about it here:

congressionalaward.org.

Military and Police Academy

Military academies, police training, and the ROTC place a high value on physical fitness. It can help if your child's level of fitness is measurable in some way. For example, measurable fitness might mean your child is a member of a sports team, competes in a marathon, or attained Eagle Scout. If your child is involved in physical activity, and can document it, they will have the advantage.

NCAA Sports

The NCAA regulates athletes and organizes the athletic programs of many college sports. NCAA stands for the National Collegiate Athletic Association. If you don't know what it is, you probably aren't worried about it at all. But if you do know what it is, then as a homeschool parent you may feel stressed or insecure. The NCAA can be a challenge, but it's a challenge for all parents, not only homeschoolers. If your child loves sports, and would like to continue in college, it's a good idea to do a little research on the NCAA early in high school. The rules change over time, and your child must obey all their rules to play their college sports.

The NCAA does accept independently homeschooled students. There may not be a benefit to attending an online school or program. The NCAA recently gave a statement that it will no longer accept coursework from 24 different virtual schools that are affiliated with K12 Inc. Apparently, there were concerns about a large dropout rate, some inadequate coursework, and grading was done overseas in India.

The NCAA requires thorough academic records, so maintain your child's transcript and course descriptions every year. They offer an NCAA Eligibility Toolkit for lots of information on how to complete the process as an independent homeschool. Families who are interested in NCAA sports should read all of the information provided, and check back regularly. Search the NCAA website at ncaa.org for the word "homeschool." Look at the helpful information they provide, designed to make it easier for independent homeschoolers to navigate the process while staying within their guidelines. Register with the NCAA Eligibility Center at web3.ncaa.org/ecwr3 during junior year. The NCAA Eligibility Center will determine whether homeschooled, college-bound student-athletes will be eligible.

Each year, read over every page and link provided. Jumping through hoops is one of the things all parents have to do in order to participate with the NCAA. It's not uniquely for homeschoolers, it's for all students. Granted, it doesn't look easy, but it does look possible. If it's worth it to your student, you should be successful handling this as an independent homeschooler.

The Final Exam

The final exam in this class is truly health and fitness. You know your child best, and you are in the best position to know how to encourage health and fitness in your own child. Personal fitness is a challenge for many adults. When kids become teenagers, they can learn about health and fitness the same way adults do. What are you doing to be physically fit? Encourage your child to become a fit adult.

Chapter 7

Finding Freedom in Homeschool Language Arts

Are you allowing yourself enough flexibility for delight directed learning in language arts? Many homeschool parents aren't even sure what language arts means, merely that they're supposed to cover it.

According to the National Council of Teachers of English, the five basic parts of a language arts program are reading, writing, speaking, listening, and visual literacy. That's a broad category, isn't it?! It shouldn't be too hard to find an area of your child's delight directed interest to fit within these bounds.

If you want to explore English outside the curriculum box, and you have a child who could use some delight directed learning opportunities, explore some of these ideas:

- poetry
- speech
- creative writing
- expository writing
- journalism
- science fiction
- sports literature
- early American literature
- modern American literature
- social-issues literature
- African-American literature
- Shakespeare
- literature and philosophy

You can even cover language arts around a theme, such as, Monsters in Literature:

- *Frankenstein* by Mary Shelley
- *Moby Dick* by Herman Melville
- *Dr. Jekyll and Mr. Hyde* by

Robert Louis Stevenson
- *The Plague* by Albert Camus
- Just about anything written by Edgar Allan Poe
- *The Phantom of the Opera* by Gaston Leroux
- *The War of the Worlds* by H.G. Wells

If your child prefers to talk rather than listen, look for your local chapter of a speech or debate organization, such as your local Toastmasters group.

For students who are more visually oriented, explore the visual literacy part of language arts. Visual literacy is the ability to interpret and make meaning from information presented in the form of an image, instead of text. It's based on the idea that pictures can be read. Your visual learner can explore all sorts of options within this broad category and count it as language arts.

Chapter 8

Strategies to Keep You Sane

As you've no doubt realized by this point, accommodating your child's delight directed learning can sometimes be exhausting, especially if their interests require you to drive them around, listen to them rhapsodize, or fork out the big bucks to support them. If your child gets this involved in their passion, it's important to look at the activity in the context of their whole homeschool education.

The most important survival strategy I recommend is to avoid duplicating subjects. You don't need to teach teenagers what they already know. You can let them learn it and let them love it, but don't then take that delight and turn it into something you teach until they hate it. Once you have identified what your child's interests and passions are, and they start to incorporate them into your homeschool, you don't have to teach the same subject as a school subject using textbooks.

For example, if your child loves writing novels all the time and that's all they want to do, don't purchase an additional English curriculum that takes them an hour or two every day to do; they are already working on English! Learn how to identify their specialization and record their delight directed learning on the homeschool transcript. Remember not to turn delight directed learning into a subject with grades and tests, or make it into something your child doesn't like. If you make their delight too much like a school subject, sometimes kids will backpedal and refuse to do it anymore, which is sad.

At times, parents find their children's delight directed learning frustrating, and they may feel like their child is not doing any school at all. Once you put your child's learning on a transcript, however, you'll see that not only did they cover some core classes, but also electives through delight directed learning.

Time for the Annoy-O-Meter

Delight can be annoying. But as I've said, the annoyance you feel can be a way to identify your child's delight directed learning. Ask yourself, what is your child doing that annoys you? What is it they do every day, when they should be doing school? Let's say you put a math book in front of your child; what are they tempted to do instead of math? Usually, the very thing that annoys you is also your child's delight directed learning interest.

Annoyance can indicate many things: specialization, a course that you ultimately can put on your child's transcript, or even college credit. It might also indicate something to put on your child's activity and awards list, or important career preparation that is going on behind your back. The key is to pay attention.

Annoyance Can Demonstrate Specialization

Colleges look for passion in kids. For some reason (God's sense of humor, perhaps?), the activities kids are passionate about seem to frequently frustrate parents. It's hard to recognize specialization when it is so much fun for our students, too. Shouldn't they be working? They're only having *fun*! If you are struggling with specialization, remember colleges love to see passion. They see unique specialization in homeschoolers and they love it!

What do your children do that drives you nuts? Could it be their specialization? An interest they are passionate about? Now I'll admit sometimes it can be your child merely wasting time, but if they are actively engaged in something, what is it? Put aside your pre-conceived notions about which interests are valuable.

I notice parents often see their children's faults easier than they see their strengths. A gift is something children will engage in repeatedly, over and over to the point of annoyance! Check yourself the next time you feel annoyed at your children. What are they doing when you say "Will you knock that off!?" Ask yourself, are you looking at their gifts?

I know parents who have pooh-poohed some wonderful activities because they thought they didn't have value. Some parents didn't think an activity was academic enough, others thought it was too narrow. Some have dismissed an interest because it wasn't a college-level interest, it was only messing around on the computer with programming languages. Put aside your bias and listen to what you say when you are annoyed. Ask yourself, "Could it be their area of specialization?"

Annoyance Can be Placed on a High School Transcript!

The things that bother us often become our subconscious grading criteria. Our frustrations can indicate what course work we have assigned. Think about this statement, "Aren't you done with your spelling words yet?" It indicates you consider spelling as part of their English class. Or what about this, "Is that all you want to read about?" It could demonstrate your child is working on a delight directed course, and learning without any assignments at all! Can you figure out a course name for that delight?

Then there is the classic phrase, "You

simply *have* to put that down now and do some school!" This statement can help you determine credit value for your delight directed course. How often do you say it? Once a week? Once a day?? Once an hour??? It may mean your child is spending more than five hours a week on the activity, and you might be able to make it a high school credit.

Annoyance Can Indicate College Credit

If your child has an interest in an academic subject, consider having their knowledge assessed. Even if you aren't teaching a class, the student may still be learning material because they are interested. This happened to me with my economics-loving son. I noticed that I was annoyed with his economics study, so I thought I should probably include it in his transcript. Although it felt like he read economics all day, every day, I felt too unsure of myself to give him a whole credit. On his transcript, I decided to write Economics 1, Economics 2, and Economics 3, all with a half credit value. Then I thought about finding out if he could pass an exam in economics.

This turned out to be a fateful decision. I discovered through CLEP exams that he knew a college amount of information about economics and other topics I never taught him at all! Based on test results, I revised his transcript. I put Economics: 1 credit, Macroeconomics: 1 credit, and Microeconomics: 1 credit. I gave him honors for all three classes. The CLEP exam provided information about class titles, grades, and credit value. If your child has an academic interest, look into SAT Subject Tests, AP exams, or CLEP tests to see if their annoying interest can be measured as college credit.

Annoyance Can be Placed on an Activity and Awards List

If you have a child who competes or

receives honors in an area they love, put it on the activity and award list. Sometimes parents will laugh a little about their child and say, "You're not going to believe this but he actually won _____." Perhaps the child has sold some CDs with his band, or won a huge cash prize for playing the video game, Halo, (I know both of these kids) or perhaps they win chess tournaments, like my own son, Kevin!

All of these things can go on their activity and award list, the more the better! Colleges love passion, which means they love to see a *lot* of a particular interest over all four years of high school. We may want our kids to be well rounded (I know I did!), but it also helps them to have some activities they do *all* the time. When it comes to applying for college, four years of an activity is ten times better than one year!

Why it all Matters

As your child grows, their interests often change. Yes, passion for a subject during all four years of high school is great, but you also want to expose them to *many* interests so your student can shape their ideas about a career. My son Alex loves playing the piano, but after years of playing, he realized he liked it for fun but didn't want piano to be his career. It's okay to let your children change interests and move their focus from one activity to the next.

It can be amazing when they put all these pieces of the puzzle together. As a senior in high school, my son Kevin couldn't decide on a college major. Finally, he decided chess involved problem solving and electrical engineering also involved problem solving, plus it involved a lot of math! He has won awards in math competitions as well as chess tournaments. He decided to be an engineer because of his interest in chess and math. Each activity seemed isolated until he put them together, with a straight line pointing to his college major and career interest! In this way, encouraging specialization, even when it changes, can ultimately help with career choices.

Fostering your child's love and pursuit of their passion ultimately helps them know themselves better, and prepares them to enter the world with a better idea of where their place might be. It can be difficult. It takes extra time, and it's sometimes annoying, but the end result is worth all the added cost.

Appendix 1

Three Must-Have Electives

Every high school offers elective classes. What crazy electives were available at your high school? I took Polynesian History, which was offered by my teacher so he could go to Hawaii every summer and write it off as a business expense. My brother-in-law taught Sports Communication and History of Baseball at his public high school because he loved baseball and could listen to games during class time.

Homeschoolers are not limited by the whims of teachers, or the preferences of principals or the school district. Instead, we can choose electives that are legally required, important to us, and fun for our students. There are three critical elective types to cover in high school, but the individual electives aren't the same for all homeschool families. In fact, they don't even have to be the same for each child in your family!

1. Electives Required by State Law

Each state has different homeschool laws. Usually the requirements involve subjects parents would teach their children anyway, such as reading, writing, math, science, and foreign language. That's why increased state regulation doesn't tend to affect homeschool performance. Truth be told, parents often have stiffer requirements than state laws. However, look at your state law to see what is required and find out if any of those requirements are electives. For example, Washington State requires that parents teach "Occupational Education." Other states might require "Technology" or "Computer Applications." Add these required classes to your high school class list.

Don't look up your state "graduation requirements." Those are requirements specifically for your local public high school and not for private schools or homeschools. Public school requirements change frequently and may not reflect what is important or significant. Trying to meet public school requirements can lead to frustration, and feelings of inadequacy. These requirements often stem from societal problems that are not meaningful in your homeschool. Look for electives required by state homeschool law instead.

2. Electives Required by Parents

There are some subjects you believe should be required in high school, but aren't required by the state. That's one reason looking at public school requirements can be so frustrating—

their inflexible guidelines can seem nonsensical in the context of your own child in your own home. Instead, look carefully at the subjects you believe are critical. Subjects that parents require for high school vary significantly. One parent might require Bible classes and another require auto mechanics or home economics. Your best friend might require logic, or critical thinking, or debate. All homeschool parents have subjects they deem critical for high school. Add yours to the high school class list.

Set reasonable expectations for the number of high school classes. There are a million subjects we would love to teach our children, but we certainly can't make our children learn in four years what has taken us a lifetime to learn. Each one credit class indicates about one hour of study per day. If your child takes more than eight classes each year, you are expecting your child to sit still and study for more than eight hours a day. Is that reasonable? Keep your learning goals balanced, and don't expect your child to work longer than an adult works at a full-time job.

3. Electives from Delight Directed Learning

Learning for fun can take almost any form; it's not limited by the interests of the teacher, the school, or the purchase of a special curriculum. Any learning your child does for fun can be included on the high school transcript as electives. To be quite honest, sometimes parents don't see these subjects as delight directed learning. Often, parents see this learning as only an annoying interruption.

What is your child doing when they should be "doing school"? Could that behavior translate into some high school credits? If they are constantly playing the banjo, riding horses, drawing Anime, or mapping the moons of Jupiter, it can indicate some high school level learning.

Don't turn delight into a total drag. When your child is learning for fun and you want to put that information on the transcript, the temptation is to force that subject into the public school mold. Don't do it! You don't want to beat the love of learning out of your child, or make them hate their most-beloved pastime. Don't make delight directed learning a boring school subject.

You don't need to purchase textbooks (although your child may request some for further study). You don't need to create tests. Instead, watch closely, listen, and learn from your children. They are capable of learning without any intervention. Your job isn't to make them learn; your job is to collect what they have already learned.

There can be impediments to learning for fun. If it seems as if your child doesn't take joy in any delight directed learning, look for stumbling blocks that are getting in their way. Sometimes the problem is simply a lack of maturity. Young students may need to explore more of the world before they catch fire for a subject.

Sometimes the problem is time and a schedule crammed full to the gills. If they are so busy doing "school" each day, and don't have any free time, they may not have the necessary hours to learn how to enjoy other topics merely for fun. Sometimes the problem is technology if your children spend all their free hours glued to a screen, playing games, or on social media. This kind of technology use can decrease creativity and enjoyment in other areas. Try limiting technology, and freeing up more time to see if your child can start learning for fun.

How to Capture High School Electives

Electives don't need to have a curriculum, quizzes, or fill-in the bubble tests to be included on the high school transcript. Many electives are achieved through natural learning that doesn't resemble school. Even without making these classes part of "school" you can still include this quality learning on the high school transcript.

Name each of your classes using the name of the experience: Tai Kwon Do, Novel Writing, Creative Thinking, Leadership Skills, Farm Management, Small Business, and Entrepreneurship. Calculate credits based on the number of hours worked. About 120 to 180 hours, or at least one hour a day, is enough to call it a high school credit.

Estimate grades without requiring tests. Consider how a piano teacher evaluates learning at the piano, mostly through watching and listening: watching the skill of the hands, listening to the music and the rhythm, feeling the child's involvement, recognizing practice.

Categorize the learning into subject groups if possible. Tai Kwon Do can be part of your P.E. class; novel writing can fit into your English class. When possible, exceed expectations in existing subject areas first, so you have more than four credits of social studies or music. If the elective doesn't fit into an existing subject area, then let it stand in a separate category as an "elective." In other words, "elective" might mean, "I don't know where else to list this work."

Exceed Expectations with Electives

Your job is to educate your children, and colleges want to see rigorous college preparation in high school. By including electives, you can exceed expectations in many categories. Look at the college admission requirements for colleges you are considering. Compare their requirements to the education you are giving your child. Is there anything missing? Can you exceed expectations with your electives? Include all of your academic but natural learning, whether it was intentional or mandated by the state, or even covered during the summer, when other subjects were on hiatus. We homeschoolers might be crazy enough to school year-round. We might even require or allow our children to learn something during the summer. Summer school counts, too!

Exceed expectations and put electives on your high school transcript!

Appendix 2

Tips for Families Chock-Full of the Arts

Some kids *love* the arts, and get *so* passionate they end up with multiple credits of fine arts every year of high school. You know, this is *great*! It shows your child's unique aspects, their passions, interests, and pursuits. That's what colleges love! The problem, though, is getting the rest of the stuff done!

It can seem almost impossible to achieve the balance between providing children with the subjects they love and making sure they also get the subjects they need. One mom confessed:

"I feel as though I am running a performing arts school. My daughters cannot get enough of the arts: acting, dancing, art, voice, music, creative writing, ugh! I am worried about trying to squeeze in all the important and required subjects for their high school transcripts in between all the arts. Academics are important to me and my daughters are very capable, bright and focused, but they just seem so passionate about the arts. I would hate to have them give up their time on these subjects. On the flip side, I don't want to skimp on their academics and limit their choices for colleges and scholarships. I would like to know what is required for a performing arts school, and what that looks like on a high school transcript."

Here are some tips for fitting it all into your 24-hour day. These tips will help you grab high school credit when you can, and enjoy the ride along the way!

Cover Core and Capture Delight

You want to both cover the core classes and capture delight directed learning. Be sure to cover the core classes of reading, writing, math, science, and social studies. Within these core classes, try to teach them in an interesting way that makes it more meaningful for your child. It's possible to teach some core subjects with delight directed classes, but make sure you cover the core one way or another. Once the core is covered, try to capture your child's delights and translate them into courses on your transcript. You don't have to plan, direct, or evaluate with tests or quizzes. Simply capture the learning.

Big Rocks First

Put in the most important things first, and you'll have more time for fun. Academically, that means English, math, science, and social studies. Once these core subjects have been done, it's amazingly easy to add everything else your children will love doing, and chances are they will have plenty of time. If each academic subject takes one hour, then core classes may only take four hours per day.

A child who loves the arts will be able to spend the rest of their free time doing everything they want involving music and performance. Sure, they will be busy (anybody who is passionate about what they do will always wish for more hours in the day), but they will be able to get it done if they put in the big rocks of heavy academic subjects first. I know a young man who got up early in the morning to finish his academics before 9:00 am, so he could pursue his interests all day long.

Identify Strengths and Weaknesses

It's good to be up-front about what your child excels at and where they need encouragement. Art and theater people are excellent at accruing fine art credits. They can often get some P.E. credits if they are involved in dance or marching band. They are often the kind of child who does well with English and foreign language classes. However, they don't often tend to like math and science.

So, see what your child likes to do. Then look at the subject they avoid or complain about. Even if they are successful at this subject and get A's in class, you might still consider it their weak area. This will help you take action, so you can make school smoother, more pleasant, and more effective in the long run.

Weak Areas First

Your weak area is the first thing you do with your time. It's the first thing your student does in the morning. It's the one thing you make sure is done every single day. Even when a fabulous opportunity arrives, and all the other homeschool things are put on the shelf, this is the one thing you are sure gets done. You always take the time for it even when there is a field trip, activity, or eight-hour theater rehearsal that day.

Your weak area is also the first thing you do with your money. It's the first curriculum that you buy each year and are willing to spend the most money on. It's the only thing you will be sure to reinvest in if necessary. In other words, if you choose a curriculum and it doesn't work, this is the area you will make a second purchase on, even within the first couple of months of school.

Honest and True Transcript

When you are music and theater people, it can help to think about what would happen if your child was doing music and theater in a public school. Each class would be on their high school transcript, even though there is more than one fine art per year. The public school child might have Theater: 1 credit, Band: 1 credit, Choir: 1 credit, and Orchestra: 1 credit. This would amount to four credits per year. For homeschoolers, we can divide these music and theater experiences into groups that we call classes. Make each one count as one credit. Another way of looking at it is that if your children do theater every year, and it's over 150 hours, then give them one credit of theater. If they also do the violin for 150 hours or more, then give them one credit for violin. If they also do piano, and they do more than 150 hours of piano (not counting time they spend on violin), then you can give them one credit in piano.

Hold a Morning Meeting

Having a morning meeting can help. If you check in with your child each day, you can shape and mold their responsibility index. A quick 15 or 30-minute check-in for core subjects each day can help you assess the situation and keep kids on task. It will help them so they do not forget to do school for a week and suddenly fall hopelessly behind. A daily meeting is a great goal. In practice, of course, a day will be missed here and there. We are all busy people with busy lives, after all! But if you forget a day or two, you will still benefit. If you miss a few days, you can regroup and discover any missed assignments. If you tend to fall behind, or if you see your student overwhelmed by an insurmountable mountain of work, instituting a morning meeting can be the perfect answer.

Performing and Visual Arts Colleges

If your child is interested in music, art, theater, or dance, finding a college can be stressful. College admission requirements at performing arts schools vary greatly, so you need to check with each school for their requirements. Some want to see heavy academics and even advanced math, because students won't get a lot of math or science once they are on campus. Other performing arts schools only require a general education, and their admission is based mostly on an art portfolio or performance audition. It depends on which kind of degree a student wants, and which kind of college the student chooses to attend. To find requirements, looks for colleges that participate in Performing & Visual Arts College Fairs. You can find information on fine arts possibilities at the NACAC website at www.nacacnet.org.

Help Artists Be Prepared

There are some specific and concrete steps that may help artistically inspired students prepare for any college or career. Complete the heavy academics in the morning, before lessons. English, math, science, and social studies might be best covered in the morning. Excessive car time is common for children that have multiple musical instructors and numerous performance events. Make use of car schooling techniques by getting audio classes to enjoy. For example, look at history CDs such as *Ancient Civilizations: A Biblical World History Curriculum* by Diana Waring. If this isn't a good fit, consider classes from The Great Courses, such as "The Foundations of Western Civilization." Some children are able to read in the car or speak and listen to foreign language lessons in the car. Others are adept at using their computer or tablet for video lessons during long drives. Car schooling can be successful, but don't forget to teach your young adults to drive and give them time to practice that skill.

Yes, your child loves fine arts and that is awesome! You can emphasize strengths, shore up weaknesses, and provide a strong and well-prepared academic record. Including your child's area of specialization can present them in the best possible light. Don't shy away from subjects that inspire delight! Simply be sure to provide a balance of preparation, so your child has unlimited possibilities.

Afterword

Who is Lee Binz and What Can She Do for Me?

Number one best-selling homeschool author, Lee Binz is The HomeScholar. Her mission is "helping parents homeschool high school." Lee and her husband, Matt, homeschooled their two boys, Kevin and Alex, from elementary through high school.

Upon graduation, both boys received four-year, full tuition scholarships from their first choice university. This enables Lee to pursue her dream job—helping parents homeschool their children through high school.

On The HomeScholar website, you will find great products for creating homeschool transcripts and comprehensive records to help you amaze and impress colleges.

Find out why Andrew Pudewa, Founder of the Institute for Excellence in Writing says, "Lee Binz knows how to navigate this often confusing and frustrating labyrinth better than anyone."

You can find Lee online at:

HomeHighSchoolHelp.com

If this book has been helpful, could you please take a minute to write us a quick review on Amazon? Thank you!

Testimonials

We Couldn't Have Done this Without You!

Good news from the Philippines! Our son was accepted at his first-choice school. We are so very grateful for all of the material you made available to us, Lee. How helpful the videos were! I listened to them over and over. Because of your help and advice, I was able to make a wonderful transcript, a beautiful extra-curricular activity sheet, stunning recommendations and prepped for the college exams with your help!

Lee, we could NOT have done this without your help. You calmed my fears that kept me awake at night. You were a true God-send to our lives because of your down-to-earth, effective, clear, practical, and most useful information.

~ Nancy

Calming and Practical Advice

I want to thank you SO MUCH for your help when I was panicking about getting my comprehensive record and transcripts done! In spite of the panic and the work and the time, I am VERY pleased with how they turned out with your guidance. I want to tell you that my son was accepted into every one of the seven schools he applied to, and I am sure the thorough records had quite a bit to do with that.

I certainly know your calming and practical advice and counsel along the way had a huge impact. My son received generous scholarships. I just wanted to be sure to say thank you.

~ Lois

For more information about my **Comprehensive Record Solution** and **Gold Care Club**, go to:

www.ComprehensiveRecordSolution.com
and
www.GoldCareClub.com

Also From The HomeScholar...

- The HomeScholar Guide to College Admission and Scholarships: Homeschool Secrets to Getting Ready, Getting In and Getting Paid (Book and Kindle Book)
- Setting the Records Straight—How to Craft Homeschool Transcripts and Course Descriptions for College Admission and Scholarships (Book and Kindle Book)
- TechnoLogic: How to Set Logical Technology Boundaries and Stop the Zombie Apocalypse
- Finding the Faith to Homeschool High School

- The Easy Truth About Homeschool Transcripts (Kindle Book)
- Parent Training A la Carte (Online Training)
- Total Transcript Solution (Online Training, Tools and Templates)
- Comprehensive Record Solution (Online Training, Tools and Templates)
- Gold Care Club (Comprehensive Online Support and Training)
- Silver Training Club (Online Training)

The HomeScholar Coffee Break Books Released or Coming Soon on Kindle and Paperback:

- Delight Directed Learning: Guiding Your Homeschooler Toward Passionate Learning
- Creating Transcripts for Your Unique Child: Help Your Homeschool Graduate Stand Out from the Crowd

- Beyond Academics: Preparation for College and for Life
- Planning High School Courses: Charting the Course Toward High School Graduation
- Graduate Your Homeschooler in Style: Make Your Homeschool Graduation Memorable
- Keys to High School Success: Get Your Homeschool High School Started Right!
- Getting the Most Out of Your Homeschool This Summer: Learning just for the Fun of it!
- Finding a College: A Homeschooler's Guide to Finding a Perfect Fit
- College Scholarships for High School Credit: Learn and Earn With This Two-for-One Strategy!
- College Admission Policies Demystified: Understanding Homeschool Requirements for Getting In
- A Higher Calling: Homeschooling High School for Harried Husbands

(by Matt Binz, Mr. HomeScholar)

- Gifted Education Strategies for Every Child: Homeschool Secrets for Success
- College Application Essays: A Primer for Parents
- Creating Homeschool Balance: Find Harmony Between Type A and Type Zzz...
- Homeschooling the Holidays: Sanity Saving Strategies and Gift Giving Ideas
- Your Goals this Year: A Year by Year Guide to Homeschooling High School
- Making the Grades: A Grouch-Free Guide to Homeschool Grading
- High School Testing: Knowledge That Saves Money
- Getting the BIG Scholarships: Learn Expert Secrets for Winning College Cash!
- Easy English for Simple Homeschooling: How to Teach, Assess and Document High School English

- Scheduling—The Secret to Homeschool Sanity: Plan You Way Back to Mental Health
- Junior Year is the Key to High School Success: How to Unlock the Gate to Graduation and Beyond
- Upper Echelon Education: How to Gain Admission to Elite Universities
- How to Homeschool College: Save Time, Reduce Stress and Eliminate Debt
- Homeschool Curriculum That's Effective and Fun: Avoid the Crummy Curriculum Hall of Shame!
- Comprehensive Homeschool Records: Put Your Best Foot Forward to Win College Admission and Scholarships
- Options After High School: Steps to Success for College or Career
- How to Homeschool 9th and 10th Grade: Simple Steps for Starting Strong!
- Senior Year Step-by-Step: Simple Instructions for Busy Homeschool

Parents

- How-to-Homeschool Independently: Do-it-Yourself Secrets to Rekindle the Love of Learning
- High School Math The Easy Way: Simple Strategies for Homeschool Parents in Over Their Heads
- Homeschooling Middle School with Powerful Purpose: How to Successfully Navigate 6th through 8th Grade
- Simple Science for Homeschooling High School: Because Teaching Science isn't Rocket Science!

Would you like to be notified when we offer the next Coffee Break Books for FREE during our Kindle promotion days? If so, leave your name and email below and we will send you a reminder.

HomeHighSchoolHelp.com/ freekindlebook

Visit my Amazon Author Page!

amazon.com/author/leebinz

Made in the USA
Columbia, SC
24 January 2022

54109555R00074